GRAPHIC NATURAL DISASTERS
AVALANCHES & LANDSLIDES

by Rob Shone

FRANKLIN WATTS
LONDON•SYDNEY

First published in 2010 by Franklin Watts

Franklin Watts
338 Euston Road
London NW1 3BH

Franklin Watts Australia
Level 17/207 Kent Street
Sydney, NSW 2000

A CIP catalogue record for this book is available from the British Library.

Dewey number: 363.3'492

ISBN: 978 0 7496 9255 1

Franklin Watts is a division of Hachette Children's Books, an Hachette UK company.
www.hachette.co.uk

GRAPHIC NATURAL DISASTERS: AVALANCHES & LANDSLIDES produced for
Franklin Watts by David West Children's Books, 7 Princeton Court, 55 Felsham Road,
London SW15 1AZ

Designed and produced by
David West Children's Books

Editor: Gail Bushnell

Photo credits:
p4b, Austin Post, USGS; p5tr, Photo by Robert L. Schuster, USGS; p5br, Photo by Ed
Harp, USGS; p7, Corbis; p45t&m, Falk Kienas; p45r, Andy Mettler; p44/45b, Corbis;

Printed in China

Website disclaimer:
Note to parents and teachers: Every effort has been made by the Publishers to ensure
that the websites in this book are suitable for children, that they are of the highest
educational value, and that they contain no inappropriate or offensive material.
However, because of the nature of the Internet, it is impossible to guarantee that the
contents of these sites will not be altered. We strongly advise that the Internet is
supervised by a responsible adult.

CONTENTS

LANDSLIDES

The Earth's weather is forever eroding the mountains around us. Rain, wind, ice and rivers gnaw away at the rock and soil. Eventually something gives and mud, rocks and vegetation succumb to gravity in a terrifying, destructive event.

WASTING AWAY

The scientific term for landslides is 'mass wasting'. There are three main types, which are shown to the right. Besides the weather, there are other factors that contribute to a landslide. They can be set off by earthquakes or ocean waves can undermine coastal landscapes. In some areas the removal of vegetation reduces the soil's strength or heavy rainfall helps to lubricate the slope material. The construction of roads can also steepen slopes and encourage earth movement.

FALLS
*1. **Rock falls** can involve a single rock or thousands of rocks.*
*2. A large section of a mountain might break away. This develops into a **rock avalanche** (see Flows).*

A giant volcanic mudflow, called a 'lahar', erupts from the summit of Mount St Helens, Washington, USA, in 1980.

A debris flow devastates Caraballeda, Venezuela, in 1999.

SLIDES
6. Rock slides *happen when a layer of rock slides down a slope.*
7. Slumps *are whole areas of soil on hillsides which collapse.*

A slump invades the town of La Conchita, California, USA, in 1995.

FLOWS
3. Rock avalanches *can travel several kilometres from their source.*
4. Debris flows *contain large rocks, small rocks and anything else that gets caught up. Everything in their path is destroyed.*
5. Earth flows *can be fast, like a debris flow, or slow moving. They can sometimes develop from a slump.*

An earth flow cuts through Santa Tecla, El Salvador, in 2001.

AVALANCHES

An avalanche is a mass of sliding snow (or rock) down a mountainside. It can travel many miles and reach over 300 kilometres per hour, destroying forests and houses in its path.

CAUSES

Avalanches occur when a layer of snow loses its grip on the layer beneath and gravity pulls it down a slope. There are many reasons why this might happen: the landscape (smooth rocks or grass have less grip); the weather (the sun can warm the rock which melts the snow underneath); and the snow itself (new snowfall on a frozen layer will have less grip.)

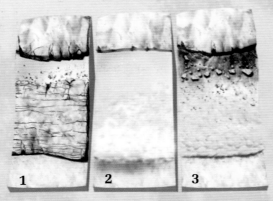

1   2   3

There are three basic types of avalanche:
1. Slab avalanches *happen when a large slab of top snow–layer suddenly breaks free.* **2. Dry snow or powder avalanches** *grow as they progress, reaching 400 km/h.* **3. Wet snow avalanches** *occur when warmer weather melts the snow. When they stop they set like concrete.*

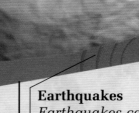

Noise
Sound waves from aircraft, snowmobiles and even shouting can trigger an avalanche.

Earthquakes
Earthquakes can trigger massive avalanches which can pick up rocks and other debris, making them very destructive.

Cornices and wind slab
Slopes on the lee (sheltered) side of the wind build up overhanging layers of snow called cornices and thick drifts called wind slab. Both of these are likely to form avalanches.

Steep slopes
Avalanches are more likely to occur on steep-sided slopes where the snow's grip is affected by the pull of gravity.

Powder avalanche
A powder avalanche on a steep-sided slope in the Himalayas, Nepal, dwarfs three climbers (below).

Vegetation
Most types of vegetation, especially trees, can provide good anchorage for snow. They can also work as barriers to avalanches. Slopes which have been deforested (ski runs, for example) increase the risk of avalanches.

THE NUMBER 25 TRAIN, WITH 56 PASSENGERS ON BOARD, HAD LEFT SPOKANE FOR SEATTLE ON TUESDAY, 22 FEBRUARY. IT WAS NOW THE 28TH. A JOURNEY THAT SHOULD HAVE TAKEN LESS THAN A DAY HAD LASTED FOR SIX AND SEATTLE WAS STILL OVER 145 KILOMETRES AWAY. THE TRAIN HAD BEEN TRAPPED BY SNOWSLIDES JUST WEST OF THE CASCADE TUNNEL AT A SMALL RAILROAD TOWN CALLED WELLINGTON.

IT LOOKS LIKE WE'RE IN FOR A RAINSTORM, MRS COVINGTON.

IT'S A CHANGE FROM THE BLIZZARDS, MR FORSYTH.

HURRY UP, RAYMOND, WE DON'T WANT TO MISS LUNCH.

THE PASSENGERS WERE TAKING THEIR MEALS AT BAILET'S, THE TOWN'S HOTEL.

THE NEXT TIME I TRAVEL BY TRAIN I'M GOING TO MAKE SURE THEY HAVE A DINING CAR.

THE HOTEL FOOD IS RATHER PLAIN BUT AT LEAST THERE IS PLENTY OF IT.

THE NUMBER 25 WAS NOT ALONE. ON ITS LEFT STOOD THE FAST MAIL TRAIN. TO ITS RIGHT WAS A GREAT NORTHERN RAILWAYS PRIVATE CAR AND ENGINE AS WELL AS FOUR ELECTRIC MOTORS AND A ROTARY SNOWPLOUGH.

AT THE HOTEL...

I'LL SEE TO YOUR FOOD JUST AS SOON AS I CAN.

THANK YOU, MR BAILET.

MAYBE WE'LL BE ABLE TO LEAVE NOW THAT THE WEATHER IS GETTING WARMER. WHAT DO YOU THINK, MR ROGERS?

AT THIS TIME OF YEAR WARM WEATHER SPELLS TROUBLE IN THESE MOUNTAINS. IT'S THE AVALANCHE SEASON, MRS STARRETT.

WITH THE TELEGRAPH WIRES DOWN WE DON'T KNOW WHAT'S HAPPENING. I HOPE PETTIT GETS BACK SOON.

JOSEPH PETTIT WAS THE CONDUCTOR ON TRAIN NUMBER 25. HE HAD MADE THE TREK DOWN THE MOUNTAIN TO SCENIC HOT SPRINGS FOR SUPPLIES AND NEWS. LATER THAT DAY HE RETURNED. IN THE HOTEL LOUNGE...

A SLIDE HAS BLOCKED THE EAST ENTRANCE TO THE TUNNEL. IT TOOK OUT THE COOKHOUSE AND KILLED TWO MEN. THERE ARE AVALANCHES AND DRIFTS ALONG THE ENTIRE TRACK.

TWO SNOWPLOUGHS ARE ON THEIR WAY BUT THEY COULD TAKE DAYS TO REACH US.

I'M PLANNING ON STAYING HERE FOR THE NIGHT THEN GETTING BACK TO SCENIC TOMORROW WITH AS MANY PASSENGERS AS POSSIBLE.

I DON'T THINK WE CAN WAIT THAT LONG. YOU'VE ALL SEEN THE BUILD UP OF SNOW ON THE RIDGE ABOVE THE TRAIN.

AND ONLY YESTERDAY A BIG SLIDE CAME DOWN THE OTHER SIDE OF THE TOWN.

I SAY WE GO TO SEE BLACKBURN AND GET HIM TO BACK THE TRAIN UP INTO THE TUNNEL.

SOME OF THE PASSENGERS WENT TO SEE TRAINMASTER BLACKBURN IN THE PRIVATE CAR.

A FEW DAYS AGO YOU WERE BEGGING ME **NOT** TO LEAVE THE TRAIN IN THE TUNNEL. YOU WERE ALL SCARED OF BEING POISONED BY FUMES FROM THE COAL STOVES.

THE TRAIN IS PERFECTLY SAFE, MR ROGERS. THERE HAS NEVER BEEN AN AVALANCHE AT THAT SPOT.

BESIDES, WE DON'T HAVE ENOUGH COAL TO MOVE THE TRAIN **AND** HEAT THE CARS.

IN THAT CASE I'LL BE WALKING OUT OF HERE TONIGHT. DOES ANYONE ELSE WANT TO COME WITH ME?

THAT NIGHT A THUNDERSTORM HIT THE MOUNTAIN. ROGERS AND SEVEN PASSENGERS LEFT FOR SKYKOMISH.

THE REST OF THE PASSENGERS PREPARED FOR ANOTHER NIGHT IN THE SLEEPING CARS.

IT'S ONLY A LITTLE THUNDER, RAYMOND. NOW GO TO SLEEP.

SOME OF THE RAILROAD WORKERS WERE SLEEPING IN THE DAY CAR. AT 4:40 AM...

HEY, ANDREWS, WHERE ARE YOU GOING?

TO THE BUNKHOUSE. I CAN'T GET TO SLEEP HERE. SOMETHING DOESN'T FEEL RIGHT.

AT THE BUNKHOUSE.

AT THE TOP OF THE MOUNTAIN...

WHAT THE...?

CHARLES ANDREWS WATCHED AS A WALL OF WET SNOW, SIX METRES HIGH AND ALMOST ONE KILOMETRE ACROSS, ROARED DOWN THE WINDY MOUNTAIN.

THE AVALANCHE LIFTED THE
TRAINS FROM THE TRACK...

...AND DROPPED THEM INTO THE TYE RIVER RAVINE.

LET ME SEE HOW THIS CUT IS HEALING, MR FORSYTH.

IT SEEMS STRANGE, DOCTOR, THAT I ESCAPED WITH A FEW CUTS AND BRUISES.

AND YET OTHERS, LIKE MR JOHNSON AND MRS COVINGTON, WERE KILLED SO HORRIBLY. HOW ARE MRS STARRETT AND RAYMOND?

THEY'LL BE FINE.

I FEEL SORRY FOR HER, LOSING HER OTHER TWO CHILDREN AND HER FATHER.

ONLY TWO MONTHS AGO HER HUSBAND WAS KILLED.

HOW DID HE DIE?

IN A RAILROAD ACCIDENT.

ON THE TRACK BETWEEN WELLINGTON AND SCENIC...

IT'S SLOW GOING, MR O'NEIL. THE SNOW'S PACKED HARD AND FULL OF TIMBER.

THE PLOUGH ON THE OTHER SIDE OF THE TUNNEL IS OUT OF COAL.

WHAT'S WRONG? WHY HAVE YOU STOPPED?

THE SHAFT'S BROKEN! WE'RE GOING TO HAVE TO STAY HERE AND WAIT FOR A REPLACEMENT.

WE NEED TO GET THIS TRACK OPEN!

AT WELLINGTON THE SEARCH THROUGH THE WRECKAGE CONTINUED.

IT LOOKS LIKE WE'VE FOUND PETTIT.

TELL YOUR READERS THAT THERE ARE 23 SURVIVORS. WE DON'T EXPECT TO FIND ANY MORE. WE HAVE RECOVERED 56 BODIES SO FAR, INCLUDING MR BLACKBURN'S.

THERE ARE MORE BODIES TO FIND BUT IT'S DANGEROUS WORK. ANOTHER SLIDE COULD COME DOWN AT ANY TIME. AS SOON AS THE TRACK IS OPEN WE CAN GET LIFTING GEAR IN AND FIND THOSE MISSING CARS AND PEOPLE.

EVENTUALLY THE DEAD WERE MOVED TO SCENIC.

ALL THE WHILE THE SNOWPLOUGHS WERE INCHING THEIR WAY CLOSER TO THE TOWN.

AFTER A WEEK SOME OF THE INJURED WERE WELL ENOUGH TO FOLLOW.

ON 17 MARCH THE TRACK TO WELLINGTON WAS FINALLY OPENED.

THE LAST BODY WAS NOT FOUND UNTIL JUNE, BRINGING THE TOTAL OF PEOPLE KILLED TO 96. THE GREAT NORTHERN RAILWAY BUILT SNOW SHEDS WHERE THE TRAINS HAD STOOD AND CHANGED THE TOWN'S NAME FROM WELLINGTON TO TYE. IN 1929, A SECOND CASCADE TUNNEL WAS OPENED LOWER DOWN THE MOUNTAIN. THE TRAINS STOPPED USING THE OLD TUNNEL AND TYE BECAME A GHOST TOWN.

THE END

MOUNT HUASCARAN LANDSLIDE, 1962

MOUNT HUASCARAN, PERU'S TALLEST MOUNTAIN, TOWERED ABOVE THE RIO SANTA VALLEY. TO ITS RIGHT LAY THE TOWN OF YUNGAY AND TO ITS LEFT RANRAHIRCA. ON 10 JANUARY 1962, THE MOUNTAIN CHANGED RANRAHIRCA FOREVER.

ALFONSO CABALLERO, THE MAYOR OF RANRAHIRCA, STROLLED HOME. IT WAS A SIMPLE LITTLE TOWN FILLED WITH FARMERS, FAMILIES AND ORDINARY PEOPLE LIKE LOCAL BUSINESSMAN ALBERTO MENDEZ...

GOOD EVENING, MR MENDEZ.

GOOD EVENING, MAYOR. IT'S BEEN ANOTHER WARM DAY.

YES, STRANGE WEATHER FOR JANUARY.

THE WARM WEATHER WAS AFFECTING THE MOUNTAIN. AT ITS SUMMIT, ICE WAS STARTING TO MELT.

SUDDENLY, AT 6:13 PM...

THOUSANDS OF TONNES OF ROCK AND ICE PLUNGED DOWN THE MOUNTAINSIDE.

LAMBERTO TAPIA, A MOUNTAIN CLIMBER, HEARD THE ROCK AND ICE FALL AND KNEW WHAT IT MEANT.

24

AT HIS AUNT'S HOUSE...

LANDSLIDE! RUN!

THE MASS OF ROCK AND ICE HURTLED DOWN THE VALLEY.

THE VILLAGES HIGHER UP THE MOUNTAIN WERE SWEPT AWAY.

IN RANRAHIRCA THE PEOPLE KNEW SOMETHING WAS WRONG.

25

MOUNTAIN STREAMS HAD TURNED THE LANDSLIDE INTO SLURRY. IT WAS MOVING AT OVER 240 KM/H.

LAMBERTO TAPIA RAN FOR HIGH GROUND.

WHEN THE LANDSLIDE REACHED THE LOWER VALLEY IT WAS 18 METRES HIGH AND TRAVELLING AT 96 KM/H. RANRAHIRCA WAS IN ITS PATH.

RICARDO OLIVERA GRABBED THE GIRALDO SISTERS.

AT 6:18 PM THE MASS OF ROLLING ROCK AND MUD REACHED THE TOWN.

RICARDO OLIVERA LOST HIS GRIP ON THE GIRALDO GIRLS.

THE MAYOR WATCHED AS A RIVER OF MUD AND ROCKS FLOWED WHERE MOST OF THE TOWN ONCE STOOD.

LATER.

MR CABALLERO, I AM COLONEL PEREZ. I AM IN CHARGE OF THE RESCUE OPERATIONS.

THE FIRST TASK IS TO GET ALL THE INJURED TO A HOSPITAL AS SOON AS POSSIBLE.

THERE ARE JUST A HANDFUL, COLONEL. THE LANDSLIDE KILLED ANYONE IT CAUGHT.

THE LANDSLIDE HAD TAKEN SEVEN MINUTES TO TRAVEL FROM THE MOUNTAIN TO THE RIO SANTA, A DISTANCE OF 14 KILOMETRES. IT HAD KILLED 3,500 PEOPLE.

EIGHT YEARS HAD PASSED SINCE THE TRAGEDY. 31 MAY 1970 WAS MARKET DAY IN YUNGAY. THE TOWN WAS FILLED WITH PEOPLE FROM NEIGHBOURING RANRAHIRCA AND THE SURROUNDING VILLAGES.

AT 3:23 PM THE REGION WAS STRUCK BY A HUGE EARTHQUAKE. MASSIVE SLABS OF ROCK AND ICE WERE SHAKEN FROM THE SUMMIT OF HUASCARAN AND TORE DOWN THE MOUNTAINSIDE, BOUNCING OFF THE VALLEY WALLS.

ONCE AGAIN RANRAHIRCA WAS HIT, BUT THIS TIME PART OF THE LANDSLIDE JUMPED THE RIDGE THAT HAD PROTECTED YUNGAY IN 1962. IT DESTROYED THE TOWN, KILLING OVER 17,000 PEOPLE.

RANRAHIRCA WAS REBUILT IN A MORE SHELTERED PLACE. YUNGAY WAS LEFT AS A MEMORIAL.

THE END

THE PHILIPPINE MUDSLIDE, 2006

GUINSAUGON VILLAGE WAS HOME TO NEARLY 1,500 PEOPLE. IT LAY AT THE FOOT OF KAN ABAG MOUNTAIN ON THE ISLAND OF LEYTE.

AFTER WEEKS OF CONSTANT RAIN, FRIDAY, 17 FEBRUARY WAS FINE AND SUNNY.

IRENEA, ARE YOU THERE? IT'S ME – LORETA. I NEED A FEW BAGS OF RICE.

IRENEA VELASCO OWNED A SMALL STORE AND POOL ROOM.

COMING, LORETA.

HERE YOU ARE.

THANKS, IRENEA. HOW IS BUSINESS?

BETTER, NOW THAT PEOPLE ARE STARTING TO COME BACK TO THE VILLAGE.

I DON'T KNOW WHY THE AUTHORITIES TRIED TO EVACUATE US. THEY SAY THE RAIN MIGHT CAUSE THE MOUNTAIN TO FALL ON US. WELL, IT'S NOT RAINING NOW.

JOSEPHINE ESPINOSA, HER MOTHER AND BROTHER HAD BEEN TO A MOTHERS' MEETING AT THE VILLAGE HALL.

WHY COULDN'T WE HAVE STAYED LONGER? WE MISSED OUT ON THE CAKES AND FRUIT JUICE.

WE HAVE TO GO AND MEET YOUR FATHER. HE'S FIXING YOUR AUNT'S ROOF.

FLORENCIO LIBATON AND HIS WIFE, PORFIRIA, WERE AT HOME.

FLORENCIO, INSTEAD OF JUST SITTING THERE YOU CAN HELP ME AROUND THE HOUSE.

BUT IT'S MY DAY OFF.

OUTSIDE THE VILLAGE, MARY BULAGSAC WAS MAKING USE OF THE SUNNY WEATHER.

IT'S GOOD TO BE ABLE TO DRY THE LAUNDRY IN THE SUNSHINE AGAIN, MOTHER.

NEARBY, SIX-YEAR-OLD ROSMARIE SIBUNGA WAS PLAYING.

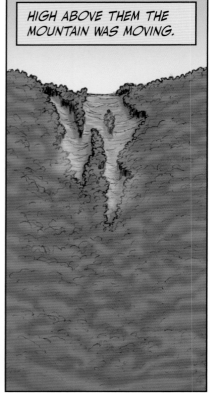

HIGH ABOVE THEM THE MOUNTAIN WAS MOVING.

SLOWLY AT FIRST.

BARRUMMBLE!

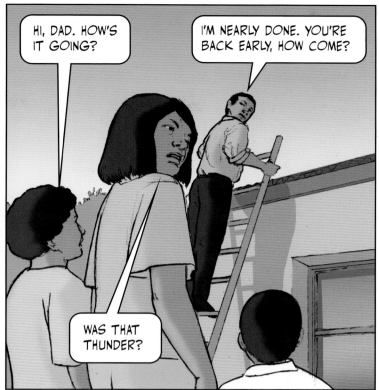

HI, DAD. HOW'S IT GOING?

I'M NEARLY DONE. YOU'RE BACK EARLY, HOW COME?

WAS THAT THUNDER?

JOSEPHINE'S FATHER LOOKED UP AT THE MOUNTAIN.

GASP!

WHAT IS IT DAD? WHAT'S WRONG?

RUN!

38

A RESCUE CENTRE HAD BEEN SET UP NEAR THE MUDSLIDE. LIEUTENANT COLONEL RAUL FARNACIO OF THE PHILIPPINE ARMY WAS IN OVERALL COMMAND.

THE RESCUERS CONCENTRATED ON FINDING THE SCHOOL.

IT'S LIKE TRYING TO FIND A NEEDLE IN A HAYSTACK, SIR.

ARE YOU TELLING ME, CAPTAIN, THAT SCHOOLCHILDREN MAY STILL BE ALIVE, TRAPPED IN THEIR SCHOOL?

YES, SIR. WE'VE BEEN GETTING TEXT MESSAGES FROM THEM. THERE ARE OVER 240 CHILDREN AND TEACHERS OUT THERE SOMEWHERE.

WE THINK THE MUDSLIDE PICKED THE SCHOOL UP, CARRIED IT FOR 300 YARDS AND DUMPED IT OVER THERE. THE MUD MUST BE AROUND 60 FEET THICK IN PLACES.

ON SUNDAY, US WARSHIPS DROPPED ANCHOR IN CABALIAN BAY, CARRYING MARINES SENT TO HELP WITH THE RESCUE.

THE RESCUERS THEMSELVES FACE DANGER. THE WET MUD IS LIKE QUICKSAND IN PLACES. TRENCHES AND HOLES CAN COLLAPSE AT A MOMENT'S NOTICE.

AND THE RESCUERS HAVE TO BE EVER WATCHFUL. ANY MINUTE THE SHIFTING EARTH COULD SEND ANOTHER MUDSLIDE CASCADING DOWN THE MOUNTAIN.

THIS IS ANDREW HARDING, FOR THE BBC, AT GUINSAUGON, THE PHILIPPINES.

AFTER A WEEK THE RESCUE EFFORTS WERE CALLED OFF.

THE SCHOOL WAS NEVER FOUND. IT REMAINS BURIED WITH NEARLY EVERY OTHER BUILDING IN GUINSAUGON. 157 BODIES WERE RECOVERED FROM THE MUD. 972 ARE STILL MISSING.

THE END

WARNINGS, PREVENTION & RESCUE

As the weather continues to erode mountains, rocks, ice and mud continue to fall down their slopes.

DANGER

Some of the dangers associated with mass wasting, such as rock falls and avalanches, can be controlled. Some, such as lahars, are difficult to predict or prevent. As human activity in the wilderness increases, more and more people are at risk from these dangers. People need to be able to recognise dangers such as cornices on snow slopes and steep slopes near campsites, as well as heeding warning signs. Carrying beepers and other safety equipment greatly increases the chances of survival, especially since it may take rescuers a long time to reach the site of an accident.

Rock falls and avalanches can be contained by building barriers. Strong netting and fences, made from steel, protect roads and railroads (above). Specially designed snow fences protect skiers from snow avalanches on Mount Mannlichen, Switzerland (right).

Signs can point out the dangers of rock falls (right) and avalanches but they can't stop people from roaming into these areas.

Avalanche guns and special systems (below) keep avalanches in check. Triggering small avalanches with explosives stops the build-up of snow which would otherwise create a large avalanche.

Due to noise and weight, snowmobilers (left) run the highest risk of being caught in an avalanche. Once buried by snow, victims of avalanches have little time to be found (below). Beepers (above) which transmit and receive radio 'beeps' can improve a victim's chance of survival.

One hour buried = 20% survive

35 minutes buried = 50% survive

15 minutes buried = 85% survive

GLOSSARY

associated Related to or connected with.

blizzard A severe snowstorm.

cascading Pouring down.

conductor A person who collects fares on public transport.

earthquake A violent shaking of the ground created by the sudden movement of the Earth's crust.

epidemic An outbreak of a disease that spreads to a large number of people quickly.

erode To wear away rock, usually by water freezing in cracks in the rocks which splits the rock, or wind and water carrying dust particles and small rocks, which rub away at the rock like sandpaper.

gravity The force that attracts everything to the centre of the Earth.

lahar A large, destructive mudflow created by an erupting volcano.

lubricate To make something slippery.

predict To say what will happen in the future.

ravine A small, narrow, steep-sided valley.

slurry A watery mixture of something, like mud.

succumb To give way to a stronger force.

summit The highest point of a mountain.

undermine To dig or erode something underneath so that it collapses.

Avalanche size table			
Size	**Runout**	**Potential damage**	**Physical size**
1 Sluff	Small snow slide that cannot bury a person, though there is a danger of falling.	Relatively harmless to people.	length <50 metres volume <100 cubic metres
2 Small	Stops within the slope.	Could bury, injure or kill a person.	length <100 metres volume <1,000 cubic metres
3 Medium	Runs to the bottom of the slope.	Could bury or destroy a car, damage a truck, destroy small buildings, break trees.	length <1,000 metres volume <10,000 cubic metres
4 Large	Runs over flat areas (significantly less than 30°) of at least 50 metres in length, may reach the valley bottom.	Could bury and destroy large lorries and trains, large buildings and forested areas.	length >1,000 metres volume >10,000 cubic metres

FOR MORE INFORMATION

ORGANISATIONS

Met Office
FitzRoy Road
Exeter
Devon EX1 3PB
+44 1392 885680
Email: enquiries@metoffice.gov.uk
Web site: http://www.metoffice.gov.uk

FOR FURTHER READING

Kerr, Jim. *Hillary and Norgay's Mount Everest Adventure* (Great Journeys Across Earth). Oxford, England: Heinemann Library, 2007.

Mountain Rescue Team. Oxford, England: Heinemann Library, 2006.

Spilsbury, Louise. *Thundering Landslides* (Awesome Forces of Nature Series). Oxford, England: Heinemann Library, 2005.

Spilsbury, Louise and Richard. *Crushing Avalanches* (Awesome Forces of Nature Series). Oxford, England: Heinemann Library, 2004.

Spilsbury, Louise and Richard. *Landslides and Avalanches* (Natural Disasters). London, England: Wayland, 2007.

INDEX